FLORIDA KEYS
impressions

photography and text by
Tom and Therisa Stack

FARCOUNTRY
PRESS

ABOVE: A great egret in breeding plumage roosts on a mangrove at the Florida Keys Wild Bird Rehabilitation Center in Key Largo.

TITLE PAGE: Mangrove islands frame a dispersing boat wake at the bayside mouth of Snake Creek.

RIGHT: Boats secured to mooring buoys at the ever-popular snorkeling and scuba location of Molasses Reef off Key Largo.

FRONT COVER: Florida Bay fisherman pole over the shallow fishing flats off Islamorada in search of elusive bonefish.

BACK COVER: This historic Key West lighthouse was constructed in 1849 and then raised an additional twenty feet in 1895.

ISBN 1-56037-290-7
Photography © 2004 Tom and Therisa Stack
© 2004 Farcountry Press
Text by Tom and Therisa Stack

For more information on our books write Farcountry Press, P.O. Box 5630, Helena, MT 59604; call (800) 821-3874; or visit www.farcountrypress.com

Created, produced, and designed in the United States. Printed in China.
08 07 06 05 04   1 2 3 4 5

Introduction

by Tom and Therisa Stack

*A*hh…the romance! Sounds of ospreys calling to their mates, the salty aroma of the ocean breezes, the textures and rippled patterns of the azure waters surrounding mangrove-cloaked islands, the mildly tart taste of Key lime pie, the snap of sails in the wind—all etch enduring impressions into the memory. The fabulous Florida Keys are a paradise for the senses.

Stretching approximately 108 miles from legendary Key Largo to the "end of the road" in Key West, the Florida Keys are a string of islands and islets hosting coral reef and mangrove ecosystems. Hardwood hammocks and sea grass beds embellish the landscape with their distinctive colors. Sunlight shimmers across turquoise bays, while pelicans glide on moisture-laden thermal air currents. Where else can you explore subtropical wonders while island hopping by car? Bathed by clear, warm Gulf Stream waters to the east and bordered by Florida Bay to the west, the Keys are truly unique.

Lying on a thick layer of limestone, the Keys are actually a fossilized coral reef, formed over millennia with the ebb and flow of ocean levels. Living coral reefs lie four to six miles offshore and protect the Keys from waves and surf erosion, while new islands slowly are being created as sediment becomes trapped between mangrove roots.

Indigenous Calusa, Tequesta, and Matecumbe Indians were first encountered by Spanish explorer Juan Ponce de Leon during his search for the "fountain of youth" in 1513. European diseases, for which the Indians possessed no immunity, took an extraordinary toll on the native population, which all but disappeared 150 years later.

With little or no fresh water available, early Spanish explorers largely ignored these islands for over two centuries. However, the northerly flowing Gulf Stream waters were the maritime expressway for gold- and silver-laden Spanish galleons returning to Spain. In 1733 eighteen vessels of a Spanish armada, carrying the entire quantity of silver for the year's production, struck the Key's reefs during a hurricane and sank. Vast amounts of silver and gold remained undiscovered until only a few decades ago. Each time we navigate our boat to dive the coral gardens, we wonder how much remaining treasure lies under the sand beneath our keel. Historical lore such as this only further romanticizes the Keys.

Less than 180 years ago, the first settlers from the Bahamas and New England arrived in the Keys. They were involved in wreck salvaging, turtle harvesting, fishing, and sponging. In the days when dozens of ships per day sailed through the treacherous, reef-filled waters off Key West, wreckers, salvagers, and pirates prospered. With typical wrecker ingenuity, lanterns were placed, at night, on donkeys ashore; seeing these lanterns, helmsmen believed that they were following the bobbing lights of other ships sailing in safe waters. In reality, the wreckers were leading the ships directly onto the reefs, where they would ransack them for their treasures. Many of Key West's original residents made their fortunes from wrecking, and at one time Key West was one of the wealthiest cities in the United States!

The Keys were first connected to mainland Florida in 1912 by Henry Flagler's Overseas Railroad. With monumental effort, dozens of bridges and railroad beds were constructed over a seven-year period, only to be devastated in 1935 during a massive hurricane.

Built on top of Flagler's railroad beds and bridges, the Overseas Highway was completed and opened in 1938 and was considered by many to be the eighth wonder of the world. This highway, the southernmost leg of U.S. Highway 1, is the magic carpet that allows visitors to enter the special world of the "Conch Republic." New bridges, completed in the 1980s, parallel the historic Overseas Highway. No passport is required to absorb the vivid palette of turquoise seascapes and lush subtropical vistas.

The surrounding waters, containing the only living coral reefs within the continental United States, have been designated the Florida Keys National Marine Sanctuary. People journey from around the world to gaze beneath the ocean's surface at the colorful coral reefs, truly a national treasure. Flat, calm summer days coupled with crystal-clear water and vast schools of fish make for world-class diving and snorkeling. Elkhorn coral forests, staghorn coral, and colossal brain coral still flourish in marine sanctuary waters. Often mistaken as plants by first-time visitors, corals are actually colonies of marine animals. Parrotfish, snapper, and grunt abound in huge schools that are sometimes so dense that the reef itself cannot be seen through the school! Colorful starfish and brilliantly hued hermit crabs compete for your attention in the midst of multicolored sponges and swaying sea fans.

Images of shipwrecks never cease to ignite the imagination and they abound throughout the Florida Keys. The remains of sunken ships vary from the ballast stones of Spanish galleons to World War II relics. More recently, ships such as the *Eagle, Thunderbolt, Adolphus Busch, Cayman Salvage Master,* USCG cutters *Duane* and *Bibb,* and the enormous *Spiegel Grove* have been sunk intentionally to create artificial reefs. These shipwrecks not only provide a substrate for marine life and corals to grow upon, but they serve as condominiums for fish life. We never tire of seeing the eerie, ghostlike shape of a shipwreck slowly materialize out of the underwater fog as we fin deeper toward it.

Many of the more than 4 million annual visitors come to the Keys to experience world-class sportfishing. Known as the "Sportfishing Capital of the World," Islamorada boasts more charter fishing vessels per square mile than any other vacation destination in the world. With a catch of choices, you, too, can land mahi mahi (dolphin fish), billfish, wahoo, kingfish, and tuna offshore in the depths of Gulf Stream waters. Reef fishing will also reel you in yellowtail, snapper, and grouper. Take your catch of the day and have it cooked to order at the islands' many fine restaurants. Bonefish action can be electrifying on near-shore flats, while back-country fishing in Florida Bay can yield redfish, snook, and the renowned "silver king," the tarpon.

For those with a naturalist spirit, wildlife permeates the keys. Diminutive and endangered Key deer can best be seen on Big Pine Key at dusk. Ospreys, gripping fish in their talons, swoop and land on lofty nests. Great white herons in breeding plumage flaunt for prospective mates. Pelicans glide in formation while skimming the ocean surface. Inquisitive manatees munch on seaweed, maneuvering with gentle flicks of their large tails. Sea turtles lumber upon beaches to lay a clutch of eggs each year.

The pace here is slow and unhurried. Residents refer to this relaxed lifestyle as "island time" and invite visitors to kickback and enjoy. The Keys are more than a beckoning vacation destination, they're a state of mind, offering a bounty of impressions to last a lifetime.

ABOVE: Sailboat at a tranquil anchorage off Tavernier.

FACING PAGE: A coconut palm frames the sunset over mangrove islets in Florida Bay at Islamorada.

RIGHT: Kayaks pulled ashore on a mangrove-fringed beach at Indian Key Historic State Park off Islamorada.

BELOW: Blue-striped grunts school around a large, orange elephant ear sponge at Molasses Reef in the Florida Keys National Marine Sanctuary off Key Largo.

RIGHT: An enormous brain coral colony bathes in the warm, shallow waters at Dry Rocks Reef off Key Largo.

FAR RIGHT: Snorkelers admire a large formation of elkhorn coral at Dry Rocks Reef.

BELOW: French grunts school in the shallows at Sombrero Reef off Marathon.

ABOVE: Local artist's portrayal of the seashore in a mixed-media acrylic painting on canvas, featuring a chambered nautilus and assorted seashells.

FACING PAGE: Visitors enjoy a sunset charter off Islamorada.

RIGHT: Mangrove islands, like Dove Key off Key Largo, provide a serene and unique habitat for a multitude of birds.

BELOW: An inquisitive manatee, or sea cow, explores the shallows off Tavernier. These endangered mammals often can be seen throughout the protected waters of the Florida Keys National Marine Sanctuary.

ABOVE: Sunrise at the historic Alligator Reef Lighthouse, some four miles off Islamorada. This 136-foot-tall lighthouse was completed in 1873 and is still in operation.

LEFT: This approaching summer squall provides a spectacular backdrop for a cruising boater at a marker along the Intercoastal Waterway off Tavernier.

RIGHT: Coconut palms sway
in the gentle ocean breeze
in Islamorada.

FAR RIGHT: Houseboats
provide a unique living
experience for many in
Key West.

ABOVE: The bold yet delicate hibiscus, common throughout the Keys.

RIGHT: Frangipanis' exotic fragrance drifts through the air throughout the Keys.

FAR RIGHT: Indian Key Historic State Park off Islamorada was the seat of Dade County government before it was attacked by a band of Seminole Indians led by Chief Chekika during the Seminole Wars in 1840.

ABOVE: Tiny cup corals, each about the size of a pencil eraser, extend their tentacles to feed.

LEFT: Sunrise at the historic Bahia Honda Bridge, once part of the Overseas Railroad.

Magnificent feather-duster worms extend their colorful radioles to feed on microscopic plankton drifting in currents.

The legendary Key lime pie is now a favorite desert around the country.
However, only the tiny Key limes ensure the original taste.

LEFT: Day breaks softly at Anne's Beach, Lower Matecumbe Island.

BELOW: Diminutive and endangered Key deer can be observed by the quiet and patient explorer at Big Pine Key and nearby No Name Key.

ABOVE: The ghostly wreck of the *Eagle* lies on its side in 110 feet of water off Islamorada. Often visited by divers, the ship was sunk intentionally in 1985 to create an artificial reef; it has since become home to hundreds of species of fish.

FACING PAGE: "Christ of the Abyss" resides in a beautiful coral grotto only a mile off Key Largo. This 4,000-pound, 8.5-foot-tall bronze statue was a gift from Italian dive-equipment manufacturer Egidi Cressi and was placed at the site in 1965. It is visited by thousands of snorkelers from around the world each year.

RIGHT: Golden seahorses frequent the turtle grass in Florida Bay.

FAR RIGHT: Lobster and crab traps with brightly colored marker buoys stand ready for the coming season in Key Largo.

BELOW: An elusive rock beauty peers out from a coral crevice at Looe Key National Marine Sanctuary off Big Pine Key.

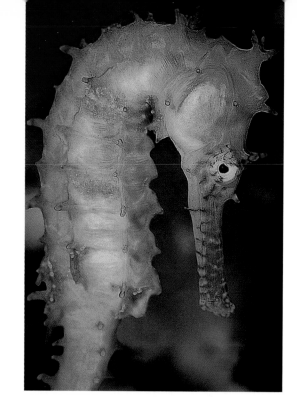

LEFT: Boaters heading home through Moser Channel under the Seven Mile Bridge, Marathon.

BELOW: An Atlantic bottlenose dolphin smiles for the camera at a Keys educational facility.

ABOVE: A giant queen angelfish sculpture greets visitors along U.S. Highway 1 in Islamorada.

FACING PAGE: Key West boasts numerous wall murals that reflect its diverse cultural heritage.

LEFT: A spectacular sunset graces Plantation Yacht Harbor, Islamorada.

BELOW: Any day in the Florida Keys is a good day—Cheers!

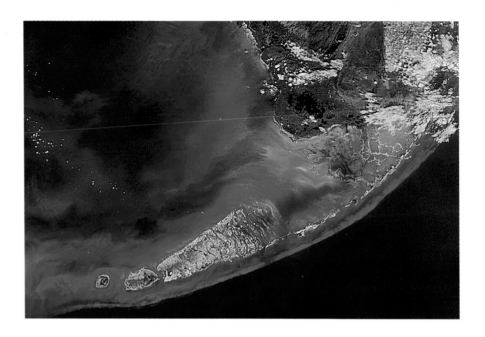

ABOVE: The entire length of the Florida Keys as viewed from space, courtesy NASA/MODIS.

RIGHT: An underwater photographer admires a magnificent stand of elkhorn coral at Molasses Reef off Key Largo.

FAR RIGHT: Historic 1873 Alligator Reef Lighthouse stands in crystal-clear waters off Islamorada nearly on top of the 1822 wreckage of the U.S.S. *Alligator,* a twelve-gun schooner sent by the government to suppress rampant piracy in the area.

ABOVE: Tortugas Harbor Lighthouse at Fort Jefferson in Dry Tortugas National Park.

LEFT: John Pennekamp Coral Reef State Park headquarters, Key Largo, is the jumping-off point to adventure.

LEFT: A midnight parrotfish flashes iridescent blues.

FAR LEFT: This pristine coral reef at Molasses Reef off Key Largo is home to a sea plume colony (left) and a large brain coral (right).

RIGHT: Children can enjoy a dorsal-fin tow courtesy of Atlantic bottlenose dolphins at several educational facilities.

BELOW: Mahi mahi (dolphin fish) fishing abounds in the Gulf Stream.

FACING PAGE: Red mangrove prop roots, as viewed beneath the water surface, provide a substrate for numerous species of flora and fauna.

BELOW: Seahorses hide camouflaged in seaweed, awaiting discovery by alert snorkelers.

ABOVE: The legs of a feather star, or crinoid, dance gracefully in the gentle currents above a star coral formation.

RIGHT: A hammock beckons, Little Torch Key.

BELOW: Millions of gametes are released, in this instance by star coral, during the annual coral spawn a few nights after the August full moon.

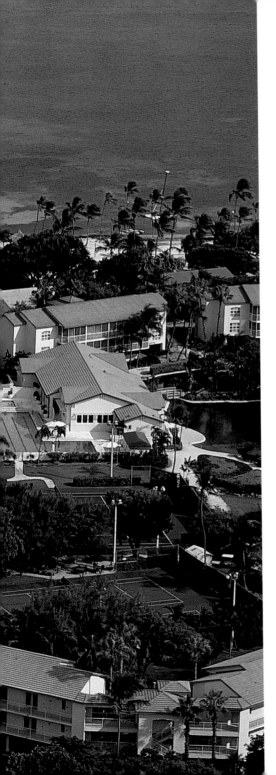

ABOVE: Exotic flowers, such as this passionflower, thrive in the Keys.

LEFT: Cheeca Lodge in Islamorada, one of many world-class resorts that dot the islands.

ABOVE: Treasure still litters the ocean floor. This gold escudo is from the *Atocha*, a Spanish galleon lost off Key West in 1622.

RIGHT: A balloonfish flashes its emerald eyes.

FAR RIGHT: Heading out for a day of excitement, a sportfishing charter boat pursues the rising sun in Whale Harbor Channel, Islamorada.

LEFT: A contemporary sculpture adorns a courtyard in Key West's West Martello Fort, constructed in the 1860s.

BELOW: The queen conch, now protected from harvest and collection, is once again flourishing throughout Florida Keys waters.

RIGHT: Picturesque sailing vessels ply the waters adjacent to downtown Key West.

BELOW: This colossal lobster sculpture is a prominent landmark on Plantation Key.

LEFT: Mangrove islets serve as both a nursery area for juvenile fish and a haven for numerous bird species.

BELOW: A giant hermit crab claims an abandoned conch shell as its home, Davis Reef off Tavernier.

RIGHT: In Key Largo, the John Pennekamp Coral Reef State Park offers visitors beautiful protected beaches, kayaking routes through the mangroves, and glass-bottom boat tours to view the coral reefs.

BELOW: A great white heron lands at the Florida Keys Wild Bird Rehabilitation Center in Key Largo.

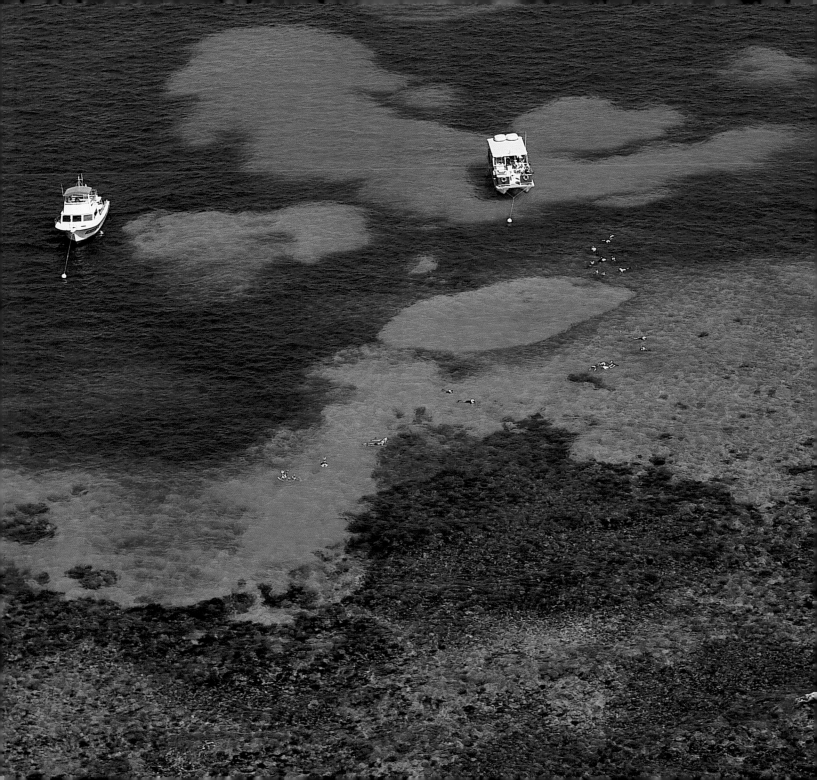

ABOVE: Delicate sea fans sway gently on a reef in the John Pennekamp Coral Reef State Park, Key Largo. Although they look like plants, they are actually a colony of animals.

LEFT: The shallow, protected waters of Grecian Rocks off Key Largo draw snorkelers from around the world.

FACING PAGE: A kayaker navigates through enchanting young mangroves at sunset, Tavernier.

BELOW: A young red mangrove has taken root in the shallow waters of Florida Bay, beginning the process of island building.

ABOVE: A cormorant rests briefly on a mangrove prop root while basking in the sun's last warming rays.

ABOVE: Once an endangered species, ospreys are now plentiful throughout the Keys.

RIGHT: The Overseas Highway cuts through Tavernier; just offshore is Tavernier Key.

RIGHT: A scuba diver explores a tranquil coral garden at The Elbow reef off Key Largo.

BELOW: Foraging for food, a southern stingray glides harmlessly over the sandy bottom off Marathon.

LEFT: An elevated portion of the Overseas Highway north of Long Key allows sailboats to pass underneath.

BELOW: A longspine squirrelfish warily erects its dorsal fin at the close approach of a diver, Looe Key National Marine Sanctuary off Big Pine Key.

RIGHT: Local personality Captain Spencer Slate coaxes a green moray eel from the wreckage of *The City of Washington* off Key Largo.

BELOW: Schooling yellowtails flash through Gulf Stream waters.

ABOVE: Ungainly but cute, brown pelicans are more than happy to pose for cameras.

RIGHT: The Dolphin Research Center on Grassy Key provides informative and educational dolphin encounters.

RIGHT: Feather-duster worms decorate coral reefs with their vibrantly colored radiole crowns.

BELOW: Peering out from the safety of its protective shell, a tiny red reef hermit crab scuttles across an algae blanket at Conch Reef off Tavernier.

A young snorkeler revels in his starfish discovery in the shallow waters off Islamorada.

*R*espected as one of the world's most widely published photography couples, Tom and Therisa Stack are full-time professionals with more than thirty-five years of experience. From their home base in Key Largo, they journey on frequent assignments throughout the Florida Keys and Caribbean. They work closely with National Oceanic and Atmospheric Administration and Florida Keys National Marine Sanctuary researchers who are actively involved with the preservation of the fragile coral reef and mangrove ecosystems.

Their photography has been published in *National Geographic, National Wildlife, Audubon Magazine, Sierra Magazine, Travel & Leisure, Islands, Travel Holiday, Outside Magazine, Backpacker, Nature Conservancy, National Parks, Blue Planet, Scuba Diving, Sport Diver, Geo, Canoe & Kayak Magazine, Yachting, Power & Motoryacht,* Discovery Channel Guides, Hallmark and American Greetings calendars, *Encyclopaedia Britannica, Encarta,* and many other books and magazines.

www.tomstackphoto.com